Award Winning Real Estate Sales

In a Declining or Depressed Market

Strategies For Thriving, Not Just Surviving, During the Bad Times

Paul F. Caranci

Award Winning Real Estate Sales
In a Declining or Depressed Market
Strategies for Thriving, Not Just Surviving, During the Bad Times

By

Paul F. Caranci

Visit our website **at www.StillwaterPress.com** for more information.

The term *Realtor* (capitalized) used in this publication is a registered trademark of the National Association of *Realtors* (NAR).

First Stillwater River Publications Edition
ISBN-10:0615957382
ISBN-13:978-0615957388
1 2 3 4 5 6 7 8 9 10
Written by Paul F. Caranci
Cover design by Dawn M. Porter
Published by Stillwater River Publications, Glocester, RI, USA

Introduction

Section 1

Section 2

Section 3

Section 4

Section 5

Introduction

Why Traditional Marketing Strategies Won't Work

The real estate market is strong and you're a fairly successful real estate agent. Your sales have always been steady and you have a solid command of your market area. But one day you wake up to find that the market has changed. The strong seller's market that you have lived in for the past five years has suddenly turned into a buyer's market. Inventory is at record highs, demand has more than simply cooled, it froze, and most buyers are waiting for the market to bottom out before plunging in. The only houses that are actually moving are those that have been foreclosed or those that are offered at short-sale, and those are selling at thousands of dollars below their former market value. What do you do? How will you adjust to the changes? Do you simply leave the business? There is no need to plan your career change just yet. You simply need the tools to help you survive and thrive in a changing or depressed market.

In order to survive in a buyer's market, you will need to master new techniques that will enable you to contract a listing and move it quickly in a difficult market. This book will help you to understand how to turn a "for sale by owner" (FSBO) into a listing by helping the seller understand why you bring a value to the transaction that will enable him to sell his property for more than he would be able to sell it for on his own. To achieve this, it is important that you **BELIEVE** that you are a value to the seller and that you **WILL** be able to sell his home for more money than he would otherwise be able to achieve. After reading, understanding and mastering this information you should have the confidence you will need to approach a FSBO and prove to him why he needs you.

But why even bother working with FSBO's? Well the facts are pretty much the same in all markets. All FSBO's are homeowners who want to sell their homes. Statistics show that only fifteen percent of all for sale by owners are successful in selling their home themselves, and ninety percent of the rest will end up listing with an agent. Put another way, of every one hundred FSBO's, fifteen will achieve their goal of selling their home. Of the remaining eighty five owners, seventy seven will eventually list their home for sale with a real estate agent.

Rhode Island real estate sales reached record proportions, both in terms of number of sales and median home prices, in 2005. The following year started a decline that has turned into a freefall throughout 2012. The unprecedented growth through 2005 not only impacted housing prices, but saw an explosion in the number of real estate agents as well. Yet, most agents, despite working "full time" sell, on average, only four houses per year. Doesn't it make sense then that FSBO's are a logical source of business for agents to pursue in a "down" market?

In this book you will learn why FSBO's **need you**. You will learn how FSBO's look at the selling process and why they don't understand how difficult that process really is. It will explain the many reasons why a seller should never even attempt to sell his own home without an agent, and, most importantly, it will show you how to explain to the FSBO the value that you bring to the transaction. You will be able to explain how FSBO's always leave money on the table by selling their home for less than it is actually worth. You will learn the various types of buyers and how to explain all this to the seller in a way so as not to come across as being confrontational. After reading this book, you should understand why the FSBO needs you so you will be able to sign the listing and handle the discounted commission question. This book also includes sample scripts that you can use when setting up appointments with an FSBO and handling just about any objections he may raise to listing with you.

Throughout this book I will provide examples based upon my experience selling real estate in and around the Rhode Island market. I have been licensed in this state since 1986 and most of my practice has revolved around it. So it is natural to site my experience as examples.

Paul F. Caranci

The principals espoused here, however, are universal in nature. While the names may change, the approach that people have toward real estate remains fairly constant regardless of jurisdictional boundaries.

Whether Rhode Island, California, or Alaska, all sellers want to maximize their profit from the sale of their home, and many experience the same emotional attachments.

The information on the following pages will help you work more comfortably with a FSBO regardless of your physical location.

Section 1

Changing the Way We View Clients - Getting Inside the FSBO's Mind

There might be several reasons why the for sale by owner is reluctant to enlist the services of a real estate agent, but the overriding reason is that he probably doesn't want to pay the real estate commission. In fact, The National Association of Realtors, in their 2000 <u>Profile of Home Buyers and Sellers</u>, said that 46% of FSBO's cited cost as their primary reason for not using real estate agents when selling their home. After all, on the sale of the average Rhode Island home, which is now approximately $200,000, the average commission is about $12,000. That's a lot of money that the seller could use to decorate his new home or lower the mortgage amount, and subsequently the mortgage payment, that he will have to make on his new home. And why sacrifice all that money just to save the little aggravation that placing a "for sale" sign on the front lawn involves?

In the typical FSBO situation the sellers are generally comprised of both husband and wife. In this situation it is not uncommon for one party to want to hire a professional to sell their home while the other party insists on undertaking the responsibility on his own. Neither is it uncommon in this situation for the couple to agree to try to sell the home themselves at least for a limited time period. But, as was mentioned earlier, the odds of successfully selling the home without the assistance of a real estate agent are not good.

Therefore, what you need to do is help the FSBO understand all that is involved with selling a home and point out why you are better situated to accomplish the objective.

Marketing Strategies That Will Increase Sales

Like most states, Rhode Island sees thousands of home re-sales each year and several hundreds of those are "for sale by owners." With a market this significant it will certainly be profitable for you to capture a piece of it. And, there is no reason why you can't secure your fair share of it. Your job as a real estate agent is to show the seller how you can sell his home faster and for more money than he could sell it for on his own. FSBOs face several challenges that they don't even know exist, and, until you speak with them, they won't know how much they need you to help them. Knowing what a seller needs will give you an advantage over all the other real estate agents that are contacting them.

Six Reasons
Why Sellers Will Want to Hire an Agent

Landvoice University, in the FSBO Mastery Training Course, notes that there are several reasons why sellers should never sell on their own. The bad news is that most people don't know what those reasons are. The good news for you is that most real estate agents don't know what they are either, and neither do the sellers! You are about to learn the reasons and that will set you apart from all the others and help you sign more listings.

1. **For Sale By Owners sell for only $.85 on the dollar according to the National Association of Realtors** (NAR's Profile of Home Buyers and Sellers). A USA Today study sets that figure even lower indicating that FSBO's sell for 21.49% less than agent-assisted sales. Worse, most sellers aren't aware that this is true. The fact is that the very concept of a FSBO implies to a buyer that there is no commission being paid to a real estate agent and therefore the property can be purchased at a discount. You see, while the seller is trying to save the

commission so he can pocket more money, the buyer is of the opinion that the savings will be passed onto him. Consequently, **FSBO's attract discount buyers**. At the same time, because most working people don't have time to search for a home on their own, **the FSBO tends to repel serious buyers**, that is, buyers who are utilizing the services of a real estate agent. Investors and bargain hunters are the people that look to buy FSBO's and for that reason, for sale by owners almost always sell for less money. Just how much less is something that has been tracked by the National Association of Realtors. The NAR Profile of Home Buyers and Sellers survey, establishes a trend that is fairly consistent over time. The results are as follows:

1999- FSBO's sold for 18% less than an agent assisted sale

2000- FSBO's sold for 28% less than an agent assisted sale

2001- Results not available

2002- FSBO's sold for 21% less than an agent assisted sale

2003- FSBO's sold for 15% less than an agent assisted sale

2004- FSBO's sold for 15% less than an agent assisted sale

2005- FSBO's sold for 15% less than an agent assisted sale

2012- FSBO's sold for 19% less than an agent assisted sale

Since the average real estate commission is about six percent, it is obvious from these statistics that a real estate agent will sell a home for much higher sellers net than the FSBO. This is true regardless of the local market conditions, the part of the country the home is in and the price range of the home. The reason for this is simple. FSBO's attract the bargain hunter; those people who drive around looking for a bargain and don't employ the services of a buyer's agent.

As powerful as this information is a seller will need more convincing than this. It's actually ironic that a FSBO hopes that by saving the commission he will net more money on the sale when in reality FSBOs end up selling their home for far less money often leaving over fifteen percent of their home's value on the table.

2. **Sellers and buyers have conflicting interests.** Sellers are trying to net the most money they can from the sale while buyers are trying to pay the least. A real estate agent's job is to create a win-win situation between the two parties so that the home will sell for as close to the true market value as possible. Most sellers really don't want to meet a buyer, let alone negotiate directly with him. A real estate agent is trained to negotiate at arms length without becoming emotional or upset when a buyer is critical of the seller's home.

3. **FSBO's have no financial safety net from future liability.** Mistakes happen! Real estate agents have errors & omissions (E&O) insurance to protect them against mistakes made during the transaction. E&O protection is not provided

by a seller's homeowner's insurance, automobile insurance, life insurance or health insurance.

An agent's E&O insurance, on the other hand, will protect a homeowner against any errors made or unintentional misrepresentations made by the agent during the sales process. It will protect both the agent and the owner against future liability in that regard. Without this insurance, an owner has only his life savings or future earnings to use in the event of successful litigation.

A real estate agent would not mention this to the seller simply to scare him any more than a doctor would tell you that "smoking cigarettes causes cancer" as a scare tactic. It is simply the truth. And, if the truth is scary, so be it! The average person will be sued an average of five times in his lifetime. It is foolish to undertake that risk without the proper E&O insurance coverage.

4. **Another reason why a seller should never attempt to sell his property on his own is the physical danger that a seller places himself, his family and his possessions into when he lets a total stranger into his home.** Is a prospect checking out your home as a buyer or for some other reason? When an agent is enlisted, only qualified prospects would be allowed into the home. Wouldn't it be comforting for a FSBO to know that, and isn't it your job to tell him?

5. **For Sale By Owners simply don't know the contract.** This is not insulting, but if you don't fully understand the

commitments of a contract, why would you enter into it? After all, when a person needs a doctor, he goes to a trained professional, not to the man on the street or the neighbor.

Some sellers suggest that they don't need a Realtor because they would have an attorney draft or review a contract for them. The problem here is that attorneys are known to kill deals because, as they should, they write a contract that covers so many eventualities that the buyer is often frightened away.

Most attorneys are not real estate professionals and often are not as familiar with the standard language of a purchase and sales contract as a real estate agent would be. Even worse, an attorney's E&O insurance protects only the attorney, not the seller. And more, while an attorney does nothing to get qualified buyers into the home he will still charge to draft or review a contract, adding that extra cost that deducts from the FSBO's bottom line.

6. **FSBO's have extremely limited exposure to all the qualified buyers who would pay fair market value for the home.** Listings in the Statewide Multiple Listing Service, signage, flyers, contact with other Realtors, virtual tours, multiple photo exposure and all the other tools that real estate agents employ will generate more activity than a FSBO could ever generate on his own."

More buyers, more demand and more money. These are just the things the seller wants, and more importantly, these are just what the seller needs. And you can provide them. The best part is that the more sellers you share this information with, the more listings you will take. If you remember, and truly believe, the value you bring to the seller, you will relay this message in a convincing way and list more properties.

Identifying the "For Sale By Owner"

Finding properties that are for sale by owner does not have to be a daunting task. Certainly you can drive around the neighborhood you want to work in every week and identify all FSBO's that way. You can pick up one of the several "For Sale By Owner" magazines that are available for free in many convenience stores and you can scour the newspaper to identify properties that don't have a real estate agency's name in the ad. But the easiest way to identify a "for sale by owner" is to subscribe to one of the FSBO services that are available. Landvoice, for example, is a company that charges about $33.00 per month and will forward to you each day, by e-mail, a list of every FSBO that has come on the market in the prior week. Landvoice even runs specials at certain times where you can try the service for a month at no cost. These listings include the address of the property, the owner's name, a description of the property including price, and most importantly, the list is scrubbed against the "do not call" registry so as to ensure your compliance with federal law. In addition, you can request the information from any area in which you would like to work. Any area in the nation is available to you. Such a service is well worth the cost and will save you a lot of time and money driving around the neighborhood searching for these properties yourself. It will also keep you out of trouble for violating the "do not call" registry.

Meeting the FSBO
Scripts and Dialogues To Secure The Listing

While you know that *you* can sell a FSBO's house for more money and in less time, most sellers don't know that. In order to convey that message to the seller however, you need to be able to speak with him. This sample conversation will provide you with the information you will need to explain why the seller NEEDS you to sell the house for him. But how can you arrange to have such a conversation? The dreaded cold call!? No one likes cold calling, but when you know what to say, the conversation flows. Landvoice University suggests a conversation something like this:

"Agent: *Hi, my name is _____, and I'm calling about the house you have for sale. Is it still available? May I ask your name?* *Are you cooperating with agents if doing so will get your house sold for more money? I'm calling because when you do list your home for sale, I'd like to be one of the agents you interview. Tell me, what is the advantage to you to sell your own home?* (Wait for a reply that will probably be something like, "I don't want to pay a Realtor's commission because I can sell the house myself.) *So what I think your saying is that you prefer to sell your home without paying a commission so you can pocket more money, is that about right? Well tell me, what would be the advantage of a qualified buyer, one who is ready to buy and has the money, to find your home out of the hundreds available, and then buy it?* (The seller might say, "What do you mean?") *Well let's take your home for example. You're selling it for $350,000 right? Well isn't it reasonable to assume that if a person has reached the point in life where he can afford a $350,000 home, then he is probably smart enough to know that he can walk into any real estate agency in the state and hire a buyer's agent for free. And let's look at all the things that agent will do for him. The agent will search the thousands of homes available on the MLS, and will take the buyer on a door-to-door tour of the best 10-15 of those homes. The agent will negotiate to make the best deal for the buyer, not the seller, arrange the best financing package that suits the buyer, Attend the inspections, review the contracts, manage all of the details of the entire transaction, and probably even buy a closing gift for the buyer. And how much did it cost the buyer? Right, nothing! And, because the Realtor is searching for houses through the MLS your home will never show up on his radar and therefore the buyer will never see it. So what is the advantage to a qualified buyer to come and purchase your home? Let's meet so I can explain why I can get you more money, even with you paying a commission, and sell your home faster. How about today at 4:00?"*

Always lead the conversation by asking questions. The person who asks questions is in control. However, you want to be sure to ask questions that you know the answer to so that you will have a ready response. Most "for sale by owner" sellers probably have not thought about all these details. Once you point them out, the seller's thought process has begun, your discussion makes sense and at this point the seller probably will realize that he needs your help. You are a Realtor that shares the same goals as the seller; that is, sell the house quickly so the family can move on with their lives, and get the most money possible. Darryl Davis, a real estate seminar guru makes a point of asking the seller, "If you were going to hire an agent, would you hire a part-time, unlicensed agent?" Well, that's exactly what the seller is, a part-time, unlicensed agent.

An Alternative Approach For Meeting the FSBO

If you are like many agents who don't like to explain all your virtues to a stranger, there is another method of getting an appointment to meet the FSBO. While some would argue that it is the most effective way, it is a strategy that will make most real estate professionals cringe. That is to make an offer to the seller to help him sell his home by himself. Mark W. McKee provides this sample dialogue:

"Hi. My name is _____ and I am with _____. May I speak with the owner of the home for sale please? Oh you are, and what is your name? Have you sold your home yet?" (At this point you may get a response like "No, but we are not going to list it with an agent.") *"I understand that. Let me ask you this, are you <u>cooperating</u> with real estate agents – by that I mean if an agent brought you a qualified buyer at a price acceptable to you, would you be willing to pay at least a partial commission? Great. My office is currently working with a lot of qualified buyers, and over the years we have sold a lot of for sale by owner homes on a partial commission basis. What I need to do is stop by your home to take a quick look to*

see if it matches up with the needs of any of our current buyers. It will only take 10 or 15 minutes, and I will not be trying to pressure you to list or anything like that. In fact, I have a new special report called "How to sell your home yourself, for the highest possible price, without paying a big commission". It is very informative and I will bring a free copy to leave with you when I stop by. I can stop by this afternoon or tomorrow morning, which is best for your schedule?"

Since most sellers won't object to getting something for nothing, it should be relatively easy to get an appointment using this method. And because 90% of all FSBO's end up listing with an agent, and you are the only agent who tried to help them instead of trying to secure their listing, chances are they will list with you if you stay in touch with them. Here is a list of some free items that a FSBO might want from you that you can use to create the free report that you offered:

1. How to conduct an open house and prepare your home to be viewed.

2. A list of all of the disclosure forms required by Rhode Island General Law.

3. An overview of the funding process and mortgage programs available.

4. A copy of a blank settlement sheet. (HUD-1)

5. How to qualify buyers.

6. Lead paint disclosure booklet.

7. A summary list of the various inspections that a buyer may want.

8. A marketing program.

A second alternative for those who don't even want to speak to FSBO's on the telephone is to leave a post card or a door hanger at the home that is "for sale by owner." Such cards can be made by any print shop or by ordering from one of the specialty magazines that real estate agents receive on a regular basis.

Finally, there are several CD packages that are available for distribution to the FSBO. The cost is modest and they can be given to the seller on a loaner basis. This gives the agent another opportunity to visit with the seller, and more contact with the seller is always a good thing. Many times, after a seller learns how much effort and knowledge selling a home requires, they will talk to you about taking their listing.

Ways to Make Money off FSBO'S Even If You Can't Take the Listing

If you have tried everything and nothing seems to be getting through to the seller, don't give up. Offer to put their listing on your website. In exchange, get a contract that ensures they will pay you 2% or 3% if you bring a buyer to them. You may even be able to offer them some free marketing tools if the seller agrees to work with you in a limited "service listing" type way. You can provide a brochure box, a for sale sign, a list of advertising sources, a neighborhood and school report that they can give out to potential buyers, and/or open house signs. You can offer some services for a fee, such as developing a marketing plan, listing the home on MLS, showing the property to buyers on their behalf, negotiating the purchase and sales contract, overseeing inspections and any other task necessary for the consummation of the transaction. This may provide you with some income even if the seller is totally unwilling to list. It will also help establish a relationship with the seller until he decides to list. Then you can offer to wrap any charges that were accrued into the commission if he lists with you. **Before engaging these tools, check with your local or state Realtor Association to be sure there is no prohibition to undertaking any of these activities.**

Other ways that you can make money from FSBO's is to offer to become their buyer's agent. Obviously, if they are selling their home, they will probably need to buy a new one. Once you have demonstrated how effective you are as a real estate agent, and explained how most buyer's use agents because it doesn't cost them anything and it saves them a lot of time, they should be fairly willing to work with you as a buyer's agent.

You can ask them to pass along to you the names and phone numbers of any buyers who look at their home but don't buy it. Offer to stop by once a week just to check in with them. This will give you another opportunity to develop the relationship. You can even offer to host an open house for them for the purpose of identifying buyers for other properties.

Once they have gained some confidence in your professionalism, you can ask them for referrals from their families and friends. The more helpful that you were to them along the way, the more likely they will be to refer someone to you.

Find out where the FSBO is moving. If they are relocating to another state, ask if they would like some information about that state from one of the local real estate agents. Most sellers will be happy to receive the information and you can work out a referral fee from the out-of-state agent. If they are staying local, ask them if they would allow you to represent them as their buyer's agent. Once again, explain to them all the benefits of having a buyer's agent.

How FSBO's View the Selling Process -
Twelve Ways to Lock Up the Listing

The argument that you might hear most from sellers is that because they know their home better than anyone else, they will be best able to show it to other people. This is a fallacy and would be equivalent to saying that because you know your own body better than anyone else, you are the best person to diagnose your own illness. Yes it **is** their home and they **do** know it better than anyone else. But that does not give them the proper training to determine its fair market value, negotiate the best deal with the buyer, and figure out all the details of the contracts, the disclosures, the property inspections and all the other things a real estate agent does. Knowing the home and selling the home are two very distinct things that are not necessarily related.

Once again, Landvoice University, Darryl Davis and others point out several common misperceptions that a seller has and these become the basis of the seller's objections to having a Realtor. Being able to respond to these objections will help you secure the listing. The objections a seller may raise with you include:

1. **"The home will sell for the same price that others in the area sold for** - This is not true because the price will depend on who is attracted to the property. If no "qualified" buyers see the property, they won't be able to present an offer on it. If only bargain hunters see the property, the owner will never know how much money he left on the table. To use an analogy, selling a house by owner is like buying an item, never opening or using it, but instead selling it at a yard sale the very next day. The people that come to the yard sale will not pay full price because they are bargain hunters. They are there because they know that if they buy something at a yard sale, even if it is brand new, they will not have to pay the store price. FSBO's attract the same type of bargain buyers. It is not the house, but the people that your marketing program reaches, that will determine what the offer will be.

2. **I have a friend in the business** – Yes, but listing with a friend can cause certain problems for the seller along the way. If the friend isn't doing the job to your satisfaction, for example, how comfortable would the owner be firing the friend? Probably not too! Further, if you needed brain surgery would you go to a friend or would you look for the best brain surgeon available? The owner is selling his largest financial investment. He should trust that task to only the very best qualified professional.

3. **The home is so special or different that it will sell even above current market value** - With so many homes on the market today, there are many "special" homes available. The market, however, is concerned about other factors. A buyer will never pay for some of the things that the owner thinks might have added value. For example, your house may have solar panels, the most modern and efficient triple pane insulated windows, and many other "green" features, yet most buyers will not pay above market value for the "green" house.

4. **FSBO's will attract overflow buyers from other houses for sale in the neighborhood** - Again, the buyers that FSBO's attract are bargain hunters. In any market, in any part of the country, FSBO's just sell for less than agent represented homes because they are not marketed properly and in a fashion that enables the seller to reach the serious buyer.

5. **The property needs a special buyer** - This is exactly why the home needs to be listed with a Realtor. The more people who are exposed to the house the more likely it will attract that special buyer. There is no greater exposure than a listing on the MLS.

6. **For Sale By Owners have no liability when selling their home** - Actually, the buyer has unlimited liability. Many times, even if the seller does nothing wrong, he can still be named in a lawsuit. The cost of defending even an innocent position can be staggering. At this point, every asset the seller

has is at risk; his new home, life savings, future earnings, and just about every other asset.

7. **All people are honest** - History tells us that this just isn't true. Owners are always leaving equity behind. That is why the television gurus always preach to their followers that their money is made when they buy the property, not when they sell it. The pros teach you to buy low, make some cosmetic repairs and sell high. Some buyers who flip houses professionally will try to take advantage of someone who doesn't have the knowledge or skills to compete in the negotiating process.

8. **The service companies will help with the sale** - In actuality, no one will jeopardize his or her license to help you. Service companies are 3rd party people who can't take one side or the other. A home inspector, mortgage broker, appraiser and other professionals involved in the transaction will perform only the job they were hired to perform and are licensed to perform.

9. **Bringing the buyer is the largest part of an agent's job** - Almost all transactions are broker coops, which means that even the listing agent needs other agents to complete the sale. Very few transactions are "double-ended" today. Isn't it better to have over 4,000 agents working to sell the home instead of steering the buyers they represent to someone else's home.

10. **The standard contract is boilerplate** - This is untrue. Every word of a contract has a meaning and needs to be weighed. A real estate agent has the advantage of using a prepared, state specific, legally approved contract. For sale by owners don't have this benefit. A licensed professional understands when to use phrases like "time is of the essence," or "the following items remain with the sale," or "the property needs to be free of all tenants." A seller who has never dealt with a real estate contract and is unfamiliar with the problems that can occur in a real estate transaction may not know enough to include such things.

11. **They will save six percent** - Sellers simply don't know that they are leaving 15% or more on the table every time they sell a home. Rather than saving six percent, they are really losing nine percent or more.

12. **I have an attorney, real estate agents just get in the way** - If attorneys are the best people to get involved in a transaction, then why are they referred to as "deal killers?" It is always a good idea to consult an attorney when decisions like selling a home are being made. But an attorney does not replace the services that a real estate professional can provide. Every seller needs the services, knowledge, guidance and results that you will bring. The track record proves the sellers wrong."

Be persistent when dealing with FSBO's. More likely than not, they will reject your first overture. Unless you reach them when they are totally frustrated by the lack of action they are getting on their sale, it may take 2 or 3 or even 4 times with some sellers before they agree that they need to hire you. Don't give up!

Talking to the FSBO
Requires Patience & Understanding

Real estate is a tough business. Yet, when the real estate market is hot, most people begin to think they can sell houses. At the height of the real estate boom in Rhode Island there were over 4,000 licensed real estate agents. This same scenario was reflected in many other states. But on average, most agents last only two years and the average agent is involved in less than four transactions each year. The new buyer's market will weed out many of the "part time" agents and only those agents with proven selling skills will survive. But selling involves dealing with a buyer's objections. In this case, the agent is the seller (selling his services to the FSBO), and the seller is the buyer that needs to be convinced that he requires your services. The problem with most agents is that they don't know how to close because they can handle only one objection before the discussion turns into an argument. Landvoice University notes that the key is to have a sales conversation, not a confrontation. It is important to establish a true rapport with the seller. Agents need to learn how to handle a wide range of objections. Learning what those objections are, and learning the correct responses to them, will help the agent convince the seller that selling his home is not something that he wants to undertake alone.

The first thing you want to do is to repeat the seller's objection. This will demonstrate to the seller that you are really listening. Something everyone appreciates during a conversation. It also buys you some additional time to think of your response.

Second, show your approval of what the seller is saying. This will make them feel safe and allow them to open up more. They will probably continue to speak hoping for even more approval. This doesn't mean you should agree with them necessarily, just that you understand what they are saying. Chances are they are not getting this kind of approval from other agents.

Third, call them by name. This is an immediate attention grabber and refocuses their attention back on you and what you are saying. Now you can direct the conversation any way you want.

Fourth, handle the objection. When you learn the answers, it sounds like your having a conversation, not reading from a script.

Finally, either close for an appointment or a signature, or continue the conversation." Don't just stop because the seller hit you with another objection. If he isn't ready to sign, keep talking.

Because the final step here is the close, it is important to be familiar with several types of closes. Here are a few suggested by Landvoice University:

1. "Many times people feel nervous just before they set up an appointment and then realize we both have the same goal, to sell your home for the most money and in the quickest time possible. So this is normal. Let me stop by later, how about 6:00?

2. What I'd like to do is to take 25 minutes to let you know exactly what you would realistically net at closing then let you decide so you can move on and make the best decision for you and your family. Can we get together at 6:00?

3. Selling your house yourself creates the need for us to get together so that you can get what you want which is to net the most money for your house as fast as possible. Let's get together. How about 6:00?

4. Having your house on the market for three months causes you to see why we need to get together. What would be better for you, today or tomorrow?

5. When you hire me, I know you'll feel comfortable that I will sell your house, get you the highest fair market

price and peace of mind too. Isn't that what you are really looking to do? Let's get started, how about 6:00?

6. Let me ask you a question and please be honest. When your home sells in the next 60 days and you net just what you need to net in order to move on, would that be just the solution you're looking for? Great let's get together at 6:00.

7. When we get together and you feel comfortable hiring me, would you be in a position to list your home with me? Great let's get together. How about today at 6:00?

8. My presentation takes no more than 25 minutes and I can demonstrate the benefits for both you and your family. What time today works best for your schedule?

9. Selling your own home yourself is hard work. That's why you'll want to see me soon so we can get it sold. Let's set an appointment now so I can help you move later. How about today at 6:00?"

Section 2

Effectively Explaining Why Real Estate Agents Are Worth the Commission They Are Paid

As was mentioned earlier, most people think that the most significant contribution that a real estate professional makes to the sale of a home is finding the buyer. Clearly, to those of you who have practiced real estate for any appreciable length of time, you know that is not the case. In fact, the hardest part of the job begins after the buyer is found. But how do you convince a <u>seller</u> of that? Well, first of all, you need to be aware of the value you bring to a real estate transaction. I don't mean simply being able to tell someone you bring value, I mean actually believing that you do. Recall back to your first real estate transaction. Do you remember how frightened you were that you might be missing a step or two? That you might get to the closing table only to learn that you forgot to get the smoke certification, or that the HUD statement might be substantially different than the one you discussed with your client? You worried about these things because you are aware of the multitude of steps involved in a real estate transaction. You know all the things that can go wrong at any step along the way to the closing table. You know that if something does go wrong, there is a potentially significant liability to you, your agency and your client. Now that you have several successful closings under your belt, the transaction no longer seems so frightening. But that is because you know what you're doing and you do it well. You are a professional Realtor and you bring a wealth of knowledge and experience to your client. All you need to do is make your client aware of that! One way to do this is to visually demonstrate your expertise. Prior to your appointment, make a chart outlining all the functions of a real estate agent. List all the activities including determining the market value, signing the listing agreement, obtaining the zoning and tax information, listing the home in the MLS, staging the home for a quicker sale at a higher price, contacting your list of buyers, contacting other agents who are active in the area, placing the listing of the home on your website and other websites, advertising in the various real estate magazines and newspapers, scheduling and hosting open houses, receiving and responding to phone calls in such a way as to make the caller want to see the house, scheduling showing appointments, continuously analyzing the market to see what the competition is and reporting any new competition to the market as well as adjusting your marketing program to account for those changes, receiving offers and qualifying buyers, writing counter offers, negotiating the price, executing the purchase and sales contract, providing seller's disclosures to the buyer, overseeing the inspections, working with the finance agent and the title escrow company to ensure there are no liens on the property, renegotiating the contract following the inspections, obtaining the smoke certification, ensuring all the contract dates are complied with, scheduling the closing, consulting with the seller along the way, ensuring the smooth transition of utilities from seller to buyer, setting up and attending the final walk-through, attending the closing, verifying the HUD statement, and ensuring the closing funds are transferred in a timely manner so that the seller will receive the proceeds check. On the list, highlight those activities in which the seller is not involved. Walk the seller through every step contained on your list explaining each step along the way. Clearly, the seller will see that most of the work involved in this transaction takes place after the buyer is found and without the seller's knowledge.

Another thing that you want to do with the seller is to compare yourself to the <u>average</u> real estate agent. Of course to do this, you must be a cut above the average real estate agent. But the very fact that you have purchased and are reading this book is a good indication that you are! Let the seller know that you have closed X amount of sales transactions over the past year while the average agent works twelve months a year just to sell one house every quarter. You are a full time real estate agent dedicated to doing whatever needs to be done to get the house sold. Further, you have an extraordinary knowledge of real estate forms. You understand how to price homes in order to get them sold for fair market value. Negotiating skills is another area in which you should compare yourself to the average agent. Isn't it true that many agents, particularly those who work on a part time basis, are not good real estate negotiators? This is not a put-down to part time agents, but simply a reflection of the fact that the more you do something the better you become at it. If you don't know what the typical buyer's objections are to purchasing a property, it follows that you probably won't have answers to those objections ready to roll off your tongue. As a full time professional that has heard almost every objection dozens of times, you know how to respond in such a way so as to overcome those objections in a non-confrontational way. Finally, what about your integrity? Is there any question in your mind that you are above reproach when it comes to representing all parties in an honest and forthright manner?

The for sale by owner will also see that your professionalism distinguishes you from most other agents trying to obtain the FSBO's listing. Consequently, once he makes a decision to list with an agent, even if that decision doesn't happen immediately, the chances are that the for sale by owner will pick you to represent his interests.

Section 3

All Buyers Are Not Created Equal
And That Will Work to Your Advantage

To most people, a buyer is a buyer. There is, it seems to the casual observer, no difference between them. But there are different types of buyers and the seller needs to be made aware of that so that he understands why it is important to list with someone who will attract "qualified" buyers only. Landvoice University notes that the first type of buyer is the buyer who is "motivated and in a hurry" These are people who are coming from another state for the expressed purpose of buying a home. An example of this type buyer is a one who has been transferred to a new job. These buyers almost exclusively work with a local real estate agent who will search the MLS for the style home the buyer wants and will schedule all the showings for a one or two day period. This is the most desirable buyer and most FSBO's will never meet him.

The next type buyer is motivated, but not in a hurry. They have the credit and motivation and want to see all the homes available. They too use agents because they understand the benefits that an agent provides to them at no cost and the time and aggravation that using an agent will save them. Likewise, a FSBO will never meet this buyer.

The investor is the next type buyer. This type buyer is looking to buy at under fair market value so he can turn a quick profit. This type person is best represented by the people you see on television shows like "Flip that House." They look for FSBO's because they know they can get those houses cheaper.

There are buyers with bad credit who would really love to buy a home, but will never qualify. They seldom work with agents because they can't get past the agent's buyer qualification standards. They attend open houses and call FSBO's all the time. But in the final analysis, they will not present an offer, and if they do, they will likely not qualify for the mortgage.

Finally, there are those buyers who are looking for ideas or floor plans so they can build there own homes. They simply want to see the home to get some decorating ideas but have no intention of buying a home. Once again, these buyers seldom work with agents because they don't want to answer all the agent's qualification questions. They do, however, attend open houses and stop by the FSBO's.

These are the very reasons why FSBO's stay on the market so long and when they do sell, they sell for less money than those homes sold by real estate professionals.

At this point, most sellers will begin to understand that home selling is a profession and is not something that should be undertaken by just anyone unless they are willing to leave a lot of money on the table.

Section 4

Overcoming the Discount Commission Objection

As was discussed earlier, real estate is a tough business and requires many skills, a lot of understanding, immense knowledge and unshakable integrity. These are not skills and qualities you were born with. They took years to acquire and you should not just give them away. So there is no way that you should want to work for a discounted commission. Yet, that is one of the first things that a "for sale by owner" will ask once he decides that listing with an agent is the right thing to do. But how can insisting on a full commission be achieved without driving the seller to a discount broker?

It is important to change the seller's focus from wanting to hire the cheapest real estate agent he can find to the agent with the greatest skill and ability. In today's real estate market, sellers expect you to do more for less money. But there are only two places that a real estate professional's money can come from; overhead or profit. Since you can't cut profit without dramatically altering your lifestyle, it should be obvious to the seller that you will most likely try to reduce overhead. Yet, the overhead costs such as marketing, education, new electronic selling methods, etc., are the very things that enable you to provide the best representation possible to the seller. What does that say of the discount brokerage?

First, you have to establish your value to the seller and to do this you will need to improve your listing conversation. What really matters to the seller is how much he nets from the sale. With that in mind, the commission conversation actually begins before you enter the house. It's all about attitude. You will need to know the information inside and out as if you were reading from a script. But you will want to throw the script away and speak to the seller directly from the heart so that he will be able to feel the sincerity. For there to be sincerity, you really need to believe that what you are saying is true and not simply a line to hook the seller in.

You must believe that:

1. You are worth the commission you are requesting, and

2. The seller should not be selling on his own.

Once you are convinced of your value, you need to establish your price and stick to it. There is truth to the statement that FSBO's don't care about the real estate agent's skills or the agency you work for, they simply have to be convinced of the real estate agent's value to selling his home. One of the agents in my former real estate agency always answered the seller's question "how much will you charge me?" by saying, "As much as I can get! Now let me tell you why I'm worth it." This may be a little bold and I'm not suggesting that you say this, but it does indicate the confidence that he had in his ability to sell the client's home. A more typical conversation with the seller should include a familiarization with the Statewide MLS system. Explain how it works and bring printouts of several homes on the market and sort them by neighborhood and then by price. Explain what days on the market means to the seller in terms of how much it will cost him to carry this house month after month. Show him how, through your intense marketing plan, you can sell the home faster. Explain the pitfalls of not pricing the home realistically and the difference between pricing the home for what the seller needs to net vs. what the house is really worth in today's market.

A dialogue with a seller might go something like this: *"Mr. Smith, it is probable that the type of buyer your home will attract will be married couples, those with a couple of kids and with two working spouses. But this kind of buyer will never see your home because he doesn't have the time to look at houses himself. He will hire a real estate agent to look for houses for him using the MLS, and an agent will never find your house because it isn't listed on the MLS. The fact is that the absolute best type of buyer I can bring to you is someone who is relocating, and do you know why? The answer is because that buyer is in a hurry to purchase something. A relocating buyer will never see your property either because he also works with real estate agents. In fact, the average qualified buyer doesn't have time to visit FSBO's. It is easier for a qualified buyer to call a real estate agent and have an agent do all the work for him for free. I'm not telling you this simply because I am trying to get your listing. Even if you don't like me, list with someone else, but you do need to have your property listed on the MLS if you want to get it sold fast and for the highest price. You have a great home here, but a qualified buyer will never see your home. And do you know what else Mr. Smith? Getting on the list is just the start. You will also need to get a good place on the list. You mentioned that you were willing to pay 1 or 2 % to me or another agent who brings a buyer to you. Instead of paying 2% to have all the remaining agents work against you, why not pay a little extra and have all the licensed real estate agents in the state working for you?"*

Do you agree that this argument might be persuasive? You can continue, *"Mr. Smith, when you list your home for sale by owner, you attract sellers looking for a bargain. For sale by owners represent the Hyundai of home selling. Attract the Ferrari buyers! You don't want bargain hunters looking at your home, you want people who can afford to pay what your home is worth. Agents simply have more resources to get the highest price for your property. If only one or two people look at your home, how can you be sure that you are getting the best price? By reaching more buyers, we can be sure that when we receive an offer it will be the highest price the market will endure. Isn't that what you really want? I have over 20 different marketing tools. Let me share those with you....*

47

*Mr. Smith, if you were fishing, do you think you would catch more fish throwing a single line in the water or using a net? My marketing system is like a net. I **will** get you more buyers."*

Another approach is to explain to the seller all the costs involved in running your business. While some seller's would insist that your business costs are your business and not his concern, most will appreciate that out of that $12,000 commission, you will probably see a net profit of only $2,000. A typical dialogue might sound like this: *"Mr. Smith, 50% of the commission I charge goes to my broker and the co-broker. Another 25% goes to the co-broking agent. About 33% of the remainder of the commission that I charge goes to paying overhead fees and advertising expenses. Another large chunk of the commission is spent on taxes. The remainder of the commission, about $1,350, is my "incentive" to do a good job. If this portion of the commission were reduced, any agent would be inclined to pay more attention to other listings that pay a higher commission and less attention to getting your home sold. What do you think the motivation of the discount broker might be to sell the home for the most money possible? The incentive would be to try to sell it fast to the first person that makes an offer even if that is not the best price that he could get you for the property. Lowering the commission is tantamount to penalizing me for trying to get the most money for you. It's been said that if you pay peanuts, you get monkeys. Put another way, you get what you pay for. If you want an agent to provide all the services outlined on the task sheet that you reviewed, then you shouldn't mind paying a fair price for that service. After all, Mr. Smith, if you needed heart surgery, you wouldn't negotiate the doctor's fee, would you? In fact, cost probably wouldn't really matter to you very much at all. The important thing is that you get* *the best professional to do the job right. Well, certainly your home isn't as important as your health, but it is the largest financial investment you will have in your lifetime. So why risk that investment by hiring a less qualified professional, just because he is willing to charge you a little less up front? Mr. Smith, I only get paid if I sell your home and you are only going to agree to a sale if I bring a buyer that will pay you a fair market price. If I don't do the job for you, you will not have to pay me a dime. So really, what do you have to lose?*

As Darryl Davis points out in his seminars, "When the seller's issue between hiring you and another broker is only 1%, then you need only prove to the seller that you are 1% better." There is always someone who will be willing to work for less, but you shouldn't compete for the listing based on price, you should compete based on your knowledge and skill sets. Darryl Davis puts it this way: "If an agent is so willing to give their commission away just so he can get the listing; commission money that they will have to work very hard for, then how much faster will that person be willing to give away the seller's money just to make the sale?"

Making the strategies described above successful is predicated on the fact that you know your competition. You should be able to explain to the seller what the average days-on-market figure is in the state and how long **your** properties stay on the market. You should know the ratio of **your** listing price to the sales price and also know what that figure is for some of the competition. If, for example, the state average days-on-market is 200, and the average days that your properties stay on the market is 100 days, then you sell your properties twice as fast as the state average. This is a good selling point.

Finally, you need to know and to explain what a 1% cut in commission really means to your pay. Let's look at an average example. If a home sells for $250,000 and you sell it at 6%, the commission is $15,000. Of the $15,000 commission, 50% goes to the brokerage. You are left with $7,500. If there is a co-broking agent, you will split the commission evenly which means you are now getting $3,750. Out of that $3,750 that you get, you will need to pay advertising and other marketing expenses not to mention 25% or more in taxes. Now if you reduce the commission by 1%, to a 5% commission, the total commission is reduced to $12,500. When the agency split is deducted, your commission will be reduced to $6,250. When you deduct the co-broke commission, your gross pay has been reduced from $3,750 to $3,125. The difference between $3,750 and $3,125 is $625. $625 is 16.66% of $3,750, the commission you would have received had you not cut your commission by 1%. That is a reduction of 16.7% in your pay. If you were to work for a 4% commission, the cut in pay would be equal to 33.3%. What would the seller say to his boss if he were asked to take a voluntary cut in pay of between 17% and 33%?

At the end of the day, if the listing is so important to you that you are willing to adjust your commission, don't forget that you can lower the commission by ¼ point or ½ point or even 1/8 of a point. You don't need to think in 1% increments.

Don't overlook the cumulative effect that making a habit out of cutting your commissions will have. If you cut your commission by just 1% on each transaction and you sell one home each month at an average selling price of $250,000, you would have left $30,000 on the table at the end of the year. Now if 25% of this amount is yours after the agency split and the co-broke fee that means you lost $7,500. Think about what you could do with that money. Now what if you have been doing that for the last 5 years or the last 10?

THE IMPACT OF CUTTING COMMISSIONS ON A REAL ESTATE AGENT'S PAY

SALE PRICE OF HOME	**$250,000**
6% COMMISSION	**$15,000**
MINUS AGENCY SPLIT (50/50)	**$7,500**
MINUS CO-BROKE FEE (50/50)	**$3,750**
AGENT'S FINAL PAY	**$3,750**
4% COMMISSION	**$10,000**
MINUS AGENCY SPLIT (50/50)	**$5,000**
MINUS CO-BROKE FEE (50/50)	**$2,500**
AGENT'S FINAL PAY	**$2,500**
THE DIFFERENCE BETWEEN $3,750 AND $2,500 IS $1,250	

$1,250 is 33.3% of $3,750
So if you work for 4%...
...you are actually receiving a 33.3% <u>CUT IN PAY!</u>

Section 5

Ways to Convince The FSBO
To List With You,
And At Your Price!

The "for sale by owner" generally becomes frustrated when weeks pass without a sale. One way to convince the seller to list with you is to offer a performance guarantee. There are many different performance guarantees that you can give. One example is to run an ad or mail a postcard that reads: *"I will sell your home in 90 days or I will buy it myself."* Now this may seem like you are going way out on a limb here, but the concept is simple. You write the rules that go along with the offer. So you can explain that if the property doesn't sell in 90 days, you will buy it provided you get to represent the seller in the purchase of their new home, or, you will buy the home at 85% of the list price provided they have listed at your suggested price. In addition, the seller must agree to pay you a full commission when you list and not suggest a discount commission be paid. Another idea is to tell sellers that you will sell their home in 180 days or you will work for free. (Adjust the number of days based upon current market conditions and average days on market in your region.) Again, if they list at your price, list for full commission, and ensure that you will be representing them on their new home purchase, there is not much to lose because chances are good that you will sell the home in 180 days under these conditions.

Another method is to show the owner how many listings are available in his area. With the increased inventory in the MLS, it is not difficult to demonstrate that the home, if priced above fair market value, will take much longer to sell. This concept can also be demonstrated through the use of newspaper clippings, etc. Many local newspapers, the Wall Street Journal and the USA Today have run several stories in the past several months highlighting the changing market, the record inventories of homes for sale, rising mortgage interest rates, shrinking home sales, etc. When confronted with actual statistics, most sellers will understand why it is important to list at a reasonable price if they want their home to sell within a reasonable time frame. To find these stories simply conduct a Google search and print out your own news articles that are specific to the area in which you work. I suggest you bind them and take them with you whenever you are on a listing appointment. Show them to, and discuss them with, the seller anytime the listing price becomes and issue.

The biggest factors that determine the price of the home are its location and size. Although a homeowner may have done improvements to the property, those will have more to do with the amount of time necessary for the home to sell than the price it sells for, unless of course a new bedroom, kitchen or bath was added. Appraisers are more concerned about how many bathrooms are in the home, not if it needs paint or paper.

Many times the seller will ask to try a listing at a higher price for a few weeks and then lower the price if the home doesn't sell. However, the seller needs to be told that one of the first questions that a buyer asks a real estate agent is "how long has the house been on the market?" The longer the home sits, the less likely a buyer is to make a full price offer. In fact, sensing the seller's desperation, the buyer is most likely to present a low-ball offer. Explain to the seller that it is far better to price the property competitively so that you can bring in many buyers who will compete for the home allowing you to negotiate the price up instead of down. The only thing you achieve when you list a home for more money than it's worth is to help sell other properties that are listed for sale in the area at a more realistic price. You need your listing to be among the lowest priced homes in the area that are similar in size and condition.

The amount of money the seller needs is also not an indication of value. While that concept may be hard for the seller to understand, it is a critical concept to relay to him. A buyer won't pay a higher price simply because the seller needs the money but rather will base the offer on what the comparable properties in the area are selling, or have sold, for.

Conclusion

Selling real estate successfully is all about getting more listings. In declining and depressed markets, many agents find listings hard to come by. But that doesn't need to be the case if you know how to find motivated sellers and you know how to convince them of your value.

FSBOs are motivated sellers who have already made the decision to sell their property. More often than not, they are trying to sell their home without incurring the cost of real estate commissions. They think they will net more money from the sale of their home by eliminating the "real estate middle man."

They are wrong. By now you should know why they are wrong and how to explain that to them so they will understand you. Now don't put this book away and forget about all you've leaned. Rather, go out and start locating FSBOs. Employ the techniques from this book and get more listing than you ever thought possible. It's up to you now.

Additional Resources

1. Landvoice is perhaps the best source of For Sale By Owner (FSBO) and expired lead generation services in the United States. It provides daily email FSBO leads from every source available.
Go to www.Landvoice.com or call 1-888-678-0905 for more information.

2. Darryl Davis Seminars –
contact http://darryldavisseminars.com.

3. Mark W. McKee – contact toll free 24 hour message line. 1-888-574-8931 or email: Mark@stopsettling.com.

About the Author

Paul F. Caranci has been a licensed real estate agent since 1986. For several years he directed the real estate division of one of Rhode Island's quasi-public agencies. During that time he managed the largest eminent domain and optional purchase real estate program in state history. Shortly thereafter he started Rhode Island's first comprehensive one-stop real estate shop; a single agency housing a real estate company, a mortgage company, a home improvement service, a title and closing company, accounting and legal services, all under one-roof and with common ownership.

Employing this one-stop concept, Paul achieved award winning sales status earning bronze, silver and platinum awards from the Greater Providence Board of Realtors as one of the Board's most successful real estate agents. He developed a real estate training seminar entitled *Selling Real*

Paul F. Caranci

Estate in a Declining or Depressed Market and promoted and taught that course for the Lorman Institute. He also taught the real estate licensing course for the Rhode Island School of Real Estate.

Paul served the National Association of Realtors as a Federal Political Coordinator to Rhode Island Congressman Patrick Kennedy. He also served the Rhode Island Association of Realtors as a member of the Association's Government Affairs Committee, and the Greater Providence Board of Realtors as a member of its Grievance and Government Affairs Committees. Paul also served as a town councilman for over 16 years, and as a member of a municipal zoning board for 8 years. He is accepted as an expert real estate witness in many Rhode Island municipalities. Paul was a gubernatorial appointee to the legislative committee that rewrote Rhode Island's Zoning Enabling Act earning him an award from the National Planning Association.

This is Paul's fourth book.